CW00862677

J
JOKES
AND MORE
JOKES

MUNCH!
CRUNCH!

MICE CRISPIES

JOKES, JOKES
AND MORE JOKES

Written and compiled by Ben Dakin
Illustrated by Daniel Green

A Funfax Book
First published in Great Britain by Funfax Ltd.,
an imprint of Dorling Kindersley Limited,
9 Henrietta Street, London WC2E 8PS
Copyright © 1999 Funfax Ltd.

Why did the elephant eat a candle?
He wanted a light snack.

How do you fit an elephant
into a matchbox?
Take out the matches.

How do you fit a tiger
into a matchbox?
Take out the elephant.

Why don't elephants like to go swimming?
Because it's hard to keep their trunks up.

Why did the elephant
paint his feet yellow?
So he could hide upside
down in custard.

Have you ever
found an elephant
in your custard?
Exactly.

Why did the elephant paint his toenails red?
So he could hide in a cherry tree.

JOKES, JOKES
AND MORE JOKES

Why is a snail stronger than an elephant? A snail carries its house – an elephant only carries its trunk.

Why is an elephant large, grey and wrinkled? Because if it was small, white and smooth it would be an aspirin.

How do you know if an elephant has been in your fridge? There are footprints in the butter.

What do you get if you cross an elephant with a kangaroo? Potholes all over Australia.

What time is it when an elephant sits on a fence? Time to get a new fence!

3

CHICKENING OUT!

What do you get if you cross a rooster with a bell? An alarm cluck.

What kind of book tells you all about chickens? A hencyclopedia.

What did the chicken say to the farmer? Nothing – chickens can't talk!

AAAK!

Why did the turkey cross the road? To prove he wasn't a chicken.

What would you see at a chicken show? Hentertainment.

Why did the chicken cross the road and roll in the dirt, then cross the road again? Because he was a dirty double-crosser!

Why did the chicken cross the playground ? To get to the other slide.

Why did the chewing gum cross the road? Because it was stuck to the chicken's foot.

JOKES, JOKES AND MORE JOKES

4

BUTTERLY AWFUL JOKES

Two men were talking. "Tell me, why is it that when a slice of buttered bread falls to the ground, it always falls buttered side down?" said one. The other man tried to prove him wrong. He buttered a slice of bread and dropped it. "There you are!" he cried, as the bread fell buttered side up. "Ha!" laughed the first man. "You think you're smart! You buttered the bread on the wrong side!"

Why did the boy throw butter out of the window?
Because he wanted to see a butter-fly.

Have you heard the joke about the butter?
I'd better not tell you, it might spread.

5

JUNGLE JOKES

What's tall and smells nice?
A giraff-odil.

If a dictionary goes from A to Z, what goes from Z to A?
A zebra.

What do you get if you cross a daffodil with a crocodile? I don't know, but I wouldn't try sniffing it!

Sniff!
Sniff!

What's pink and grey and has four feet?
A hippopotamus poking its tongue out.

What do you get if you cross a parrot with a centipede?
A walkie-talkie.

What do giraffes have that no other animal has?
Baby giraffes.

JOKES JOKES AND MORE JOKES

How do you fix a chimpanzee? With a monkey wrench.

Why does a giraffe have such a long neck? Because its feet smell terrible.

What did the parrot say to the spaniel? I'm a cocker too.

What is black and white and red all over? A sunburnt zebra!

Knock, knock.
Who's there?
Amos.
Amos who?
A mosquito just bit me!

Knock, knock.
Who's there?
Andy.
Andy who?
Andy bit me again!

Knock, knock.
Who's there?
House.
House who?
House it going?

Knock, knock.
Who's there?
Snow.
Snow who?
Snow use, I've forgotten
my name again.

Knock, knock.
Who's there?
Eileen.
Eileen who?
Eileen over to
tie my shoe.

Knock, knock.
Who's there?
Harry.
Harry who?
Harry up and
open this door!

Knock, knock.
Who's there?
Howard.
Howard who?
Howard I know?

Knock, knock.
Who's there?
Jess.
Jess who?
Jess me and
my shadow.

Knock, knock.
Who's there?
Jamaica.
Jamaica who?
Jamaica my lunch yet?
I'm starving!

Knock, knock.
Who's there?
Luke.
Luke who?
Luke through the
keyhole and find out.

Knock, knock.
Who's there?
Weed.
Weed who?
Weed better mow the lawn
before it gets too long.

Knock knock.
Who's there?
Stopwatch.
Stopwatch who?
Stopwatch you're doing
and open this door!

Knock, knock.
Who's there?
Dishes.
Dishes who?
Dishes a very bad joke.

Knock, knock.
Who's there?
Pizza.
Pizza who?
Pizza nice guy once
you get to know him.

Knock, knock.
Who's there?
Anita.
Anita who?
Anita hug!

Knock, knock.
Who's there?
Major.
Major who?
Major answer
the door.

Knock, knock.
Who's there?
You.
You who?
Are you calling me?

Knock, knock.
Who's there?
I am.
I am who?
Don't you know
who you are?

9

DOCTOR, DOCTOR!

Doctor, doctor, my little boy has just swallowed a roll of film!
Let's hope nothing develops.

Doctor, doctor, I feel like a spoon.
Sit still and don't stir.

Doctor, doctor, some days I feel like a teepee and other days I feel like a wigwam.
You're too tense.

Doctor, doctor, everyone keeps ignoring me.
Next, please!

Doctor, doctor, I feel like a bell.
Take these pills, and if they don't help, give me a ring.

OOOF!

Doctor, doctor, I can't get to sleep. Sit on the edge of the bed and you'll soon drop off.

Doctor, doctor, my son swallowed a pen, what should I do? Use a pencil instead.

Doctor, doctor, can you help me out? Of course, which way did you come in?

Doctor, doctor, I feel like a pack of cards. I'll deal with you later.

Doctor, doctor, everyone thinks I'm a liar. I don't believe you.

DIGESTIVE

Doctor, doctor, I feel like a biscuit. Yes, you do look a bit crummy.

Why did the tap dancer retire?
He kept falling in the sink.

Why did the boy wear a belt on his teeth?
He couldn't find his braces.

What's the best way to make a pair of trousers last?
Make the coat first.

What has a bottom at its top?
A leg.

What did the hat say to the scarf?
You hang around while I go on ahead.

JOKES, JOKES AND MORE JOKES

Who earns a living by driving their customers away?
A taxi driver.

What's the best parting gift?
A comb.

What is white when it's dirty and black when it's clean?
A blackboard.

Why did the scientist put a knocker on his door?
He wanted to win the no-bell prize.

What did one eye say to the other?
Between you and me, something smells.

JOKES, JOKES AND MORE JOKES

How do you send a message in the forest?
By moss code.

Why did the man hit the clock?
Because the clock struck first.

What goes oh, oh, oh?
Santa walking backwards.

HAREBRAINED HILARITY

What goes dot-dot-dash-dash-squeak?
Mouse code!

What do you get if you cross rabbits with termites?
Bugs bunnies.

What's grey and squirts jam at you?
A mouse eating a doughnut.

What do rabbits do when they get married?
They go on a bunnymoon.

What pet always has a big smile?
A grinny pig.

How do rabbits keep their hair in place? With hare spray.

Which rodents are the most athletic? Track and field mice.

What do you call four singing female rodents? The Mice Girls!

What's the definition of a row of rabbits stepping backwards? A receding hare line.

What do you get if you cross a cow with a rabbit? A hare in your milk.

What do you call a rich rabbit? A million-hare.

Knock, knock.
Who's there?
Police.
Police who?
Police stop telling me
these stupid jokes!

Knock, knock.
Who's there?
Max.
Max who?
Max no difference,
just open the door.

Knock, knock.
Who's there?
Scott.
Scott who?
Scott nothing to
do with you.

Knock, knock.
Who's there?
Avenue.
Avenue who?
Avenue heard
this joke before?

Knock, knock.
Who's there?
Adolf.
Adolf who?
Adolf ball hit me
in the mouth!

Knock, knock.
Who's there?
Norma Lee.
Norma Lee who?
Norma Lee I'd use the
bell, but it's broken so
I had to knock.

Knock, knock.
Who's there?
Tommy.
Tommy who?
Tommy the truth, why
is the door locked?

Knock, knock.
Who's there?
A shoe.
A shoe who?
Bless you.

Knock, knock.
Who's there?
Alex.
Alex who?
Alex plain later,
let me in.

Knock, knock.
Who's there?
Winner.
Winner who?
Winner you going to get
this doorbell fixed?

Knock, knock.
Who's there?
Pat.
Pat who?
Pat the dog,
not me!

Knock, knock.
Who's there?
Dishes.
Dishes who?
Dishes the police
– open up!

Knock, knock.
Who's there?
Will.
Will who?
Will you
marry me?

Knock, knock.
Who's there?
Radio.
Radio who?
Radio not, here I come!

Knock, knock.
Who's there?
Weirdo.
Weirdo who?
Weirdo you think
you're going?

Knock, knock.
Who's there?
Mary.
Mary who?
Mary me and we'll live
together forever!

17

Who has green hair and runs through the forest?
Mouldy locks.

JOKES, JOKES AND MORE JOKES

If all your clothes were stolen, what would you go home in?
The dark.

What is the centre of gravity?
The letter 'V'.

What gets wetter the more it dries?
A towel.

How do footballers stay cool?
They sit next to the fans.

Why would Snow White make a great judge?
Because she's the fairest of them all.

What can jump higher than a house?
Anything, houses can't jump.

What sort of star is dangerous?
A shooting star.

Why did the computer sneeze?
It had a virus.

What do computers do when they get hungry?
They eat chips.

Where do computers like to dance?
At a disk-o.

Why did the doctor tiptoe past the medicine cabinet?
Because she didn't want to wake the sleeping pills.

Why did the barber win the race?
Because he took a short cut.

Why did the boy throw the clock out of the window?
He wanted to see time fly.

What kind of flowers grow between your nose and your chin?
Tulips.

What do you call a penguin whose best friends have left him?
Ice-olated.

What animal carries an umbrella?
A rain-deer.

What's small and cuddly and bright purple?
A koala holding its breath.

What's brown, has four legs and is found in Alaska?
A lost camel.

Why do birds fly south?
Because it's too far to walk.

Why did the bees go on strike?
For more honey and shorter flowers.

What bird can be heard at mealtimes?
A swallow.

GULP!

JOKES, JOKES AND MORE JOKES

What's black and shiny, lives in
a tree and is very dangerous?
A crow with a machine gun.

What's black and white and black
and white and black and white?
A penguin rolling downhill.

EEK!

What's black and white and
found in Africa every summer?
A penguin on holiday.

What do you
call a sleeping
prehistoric animal?
A dino-snore.

What do birds need when they get sick?
Tweetment.

What does a bee use to brush its hair?
A honeycomb.

What do you get if you cross a wolf with an egg?
A very hairy omelette.

What do you get if you cross a kangaroo with a sheep?
A woolly jumper.

FAR AND WIDE

What kind of umbrella does a
Russian carry when it's raining?
A wet one.

What travels around the
world but stays in a corner?
A stamp.

What did the alien say to the books?
Take me to your reader!

What did the stamp say to the envelope?
Stick with me and we'll go places.

What's the brainiest mountain in the world?
Mount Cleverest.

What is an astronaut's
favourite part of a computer?
The space bar.

Knock, knock.
Who's there?
Alaska.
Alaska who?
Alaska again,
please let me in.

CLICK!
CLICK!
CLICK!
CLICK!

JOKES, JOKES
AND MORE JOKES

23

What two things can't you have for breakfast?
Lunch and dinner.

Which months have 28 days?
All of them.

What's at the end of everything?
The letter 'G'.

JOKES, JOKES AND MORE JOKES

Why isn't your nose 12 inches long?
Because then it would be a foot!

There are three kinds of people in the world –
those who cun count and those who can't!

What time do you go to the dentist?
Tooth-hurty.

JOKES, JOKES
AND MORE JOKES

What has four eyes but no face?
Mississippi.

What are the two words with the most letters?
Post Office.

Which two letters of the alphabet contain nothing?
M-T.

Why is it dangerous to put the letter 'M' in the refrigerator? Because it turns ice into mice.

How do you spell 'frozen water' with three letters?
I-C-E.

Why is the letter 'G' scary?
It turns a host into a ghost.

What letter is found in cups?

'T'.

What do you call a surgeon with eight arms?

A doctopus.

STRINGING YOU ALONG

Three pieces of string went to a restaurant for supper. The first piece of string walked in and the waiter asked, "Are you a string?" "Yes," the string replied, so the waiter said, "I'm sorry, we don't serve pieces of string." Undeterred, the second string tried to get a table, but the waiter refused to serve him saying, "I'm sorry, we just don't serve string." So the third string tied himself in a knot and frayed the end. He walked into the restaurant and when the waiter asked, "Are you a string?" he calmly replied, "No, I'm a frayed knot."

JOKES, JOKES
AND MORE JOKES

28

What do you call a fairy that doesn't take baths?
Stinkerbell.

PONG!

What do you say to a skeleton going on vacation?
Bone Voyage!

What streets do ghosts haunt?
Dead ends.

What exams do young witches have to pass?
Spell-ing tests.

What do witches ask for in hotels?
Broom service.

Which fly makes films?
Steven Spielbug.

What do you call a fly with no wings?
A walk.

What do ghosts take
for bad colds?
Coffin drops.

What do witches wear on their hair?
Scare spray.

Why don't bats live alone?
They like to hang around with their friends.

Why did the one-eyed
monster stop teaching?
He only had one pupil.

A snail was returning home late one night and had to cut through a dark alleyway. As he was going down it, he was mugged by two slugs. At the police station, a policeman asked him, "Can you give me a description of your attackers?" The snail pondered this for a moment, and then replied, "I'm not sure...it all happened so quickly."

What do vampires learn at school? The alpha-bat!

How does a girl vampire flirt with a boy vampire? By batting her eyelids.

Why did the skeleton play the piano? He didn't have any organs.

31

KNOCK, KNOCK!

Knock, knock.
Who's there?
Justin.
Justin who?
Justin time for supper.

Knock, knock.
Who's there?
Little old lady.
Little old lady who?
I didn't know you
could yodel.

Knock, knock.
Who's there?
Sarah.
Sarah who?
Sarah doctor in
the house?

Knock, knock.
Who's there?
Leaf.
Leaf who?
Leaf me alone!

Knock, knock.
Who's there?
Accordion.
Accordion who?
Accordion to the
forecast, it's going
to rain tomorrow.

Knock, knock.
Who's there?
Wooden shoe.
Wooden shoe who?
Wooden shoe like
to know!

Knock, knock!
Who's there?
Boo.
Boo who?
Stop crying, it's
just a joke!

Knock, knock.
Who's there?
Irish.
Irish who?
Irish I had a million pounds.

Knock, knock.
Who's there?
Despair.
Despair who?
Despair tyre is flat.

Knock, knock.
Who's there?
Ben.
Ben who?
Ben knocking on your
door all afternoon!

Knock, knock.
Who's there?
Closure.
Closure who?
Closure mouth when
you're eating!

Knock, knock.
Who's there?
Woody.
Woody who?
Woody you want?

Knock, knock.
Who's there?
Icy.
Icy who?
Icy your underwear!

Knock, knock.
Who's there?
Ice cream soda.
Ice cream soda who?
Ice cream soda
neighbours wake up.

Knock, knock.
Who's there?
MP.
MP who?
My glass is MP.
Can you get me
some water?

ANY QUESTIONS?

Why was a fence put around the cemetery?
People were dying to get in.

Why don't mountains get cold in the winter?
They wear snowcaps.

When is a car not a car?
When it turns into a garage.

If Mr and Mrs Bigger had a baby, who would be the biggest of the three?
The baby, because he's a little Bigger.

What's the hardest thing about falling out of bed?
The floor.

What always falls without getting hurt?
Rain.

What is full of holes yet can still hold water?
A sponge.

What goes ha, ha, ha, bonk?
Someone laughing their head off.

Which is the fastest, hot or cold?
Hot – you can catch a cold.

What is Father Christmas's wife called?
Mary Christmas.

What do you get if you cross a Spice Girl with a Chinese takeaway?
Egg fried Spice.

What is tall, sweet and French?
The trifle tower.

Which letters are not in the alphabet?
The ones in the letter box.

What's the world's longest word?
Smiles, because there's a mile between the first and last letters!

Why was the Boy Scout dizzy?
He'd done too many good turns.

What's brown and yellow and moves at 125 miles per hour?
A train driver's egg sandwich.

BURP!

Who burped at the Big Bad Wolf?
Little Rude Riding Hood.

FUNNY FRUIT AND VEG

Why did the orange stop in the middle of the road?
Because it ran out of juice.

The tomato family were walking home. The son was walking slowly behind, so his dad yelled to him, "Ketchup, son!"

What do you call two rows of cabbages on a road?
A dual cabbageway.

What's round, white and giggles?
A tickled onion.

Why did the apple go out with the fig?
Because it couldn't find a date.

What kind of key opens a banana?
A monkey.

What do you give an injured lemon?
Lemon aid.

A man walks into his doctor's surgery. He has a cucumber up his nose, a carrot in his left ear and a banana in his right ear. "What's the matter with me?" he asked. "You're not eating properly," the doctor replied.

How do you know carrots are good for your eyes?
Because you never see rabbits wearing glasses.

A banana walks into a pub and the barman says,
"Sorry, but we don't serve food in here."

What did the salad
cream say to the salad?
"Shut the door,
I'm dressing!"

Knock, knock.
Who's there?
Banana.
Banana who?
Knock, knock.
Who's there?
Banana.
Banana who?
Knock, knock.
Who's there?
Orange.
Orange who?
Orange you glad I didn't say banana?

What did the grape do
when it got stepped on?
It let out a little wine.

How can you tell if a
calendar is popular?
It has a lot of dates.

What room can you never enter?
A mushroom.

What do you get if you cross a strawberry with a road?
A traffic jam.

Why did the man drag a cabbage on a lead?
He thought it was a collie.

What did the banana do when the monkey chased it?
The banana split.

What's purple, 10,000 km long and 12 m high?
The Grape Wall of China.

What can a whole orange do that half an orange can never do?
Look round.

Why was the mushroom always invited to parties?
Because he was a fun guy to have around!

What is orange and keeps falling off walls?
Humpty Pumpkin.

I SEA SOMETHING FISHY

JOKES, JOKES AND MORE JOKES

What part of a fish weighs the most?
The scales.

Why did the crab get arrested?
He was always pinching things.

What do whales eat?
Fish and ships.

If you drop a white hat into the
Red Sea, what does it become?
Wet.

Where would you weigh a whale?
At a whale-weigh station.

What do mermaids
have on toast?
Mermerlade.

How do electric eels taste?
Shocking.

Why did the fish cross the sea?
To get to the other tide.

What kind of lights did Noah use on the ark?
Floodlights.

How did Noah build the ark?
He studied ark-eology.

How do you stop a fish from smelling?
Cut its nose off.

Why did the fish cross the river?
To get to its school.

What is a frog's favourite sweet?
A lollyhop.

Who was the first
underwater spy?
James Pond.

What kind of fish go to heaven?
Angel fish.

What fish never swim?
Dead fish.

What do frogs like to drink?
Croaka-Cola.

Why do fish live in saltwater?
Because pepper makes them sneeze.

UDDERLY HILARIOUS JOKES

What do you call
a sleeping cow?
A bulldozer.

What kind of ties do pigs wear?
Pigsties.

Why did the ram run over the cliff?
He didn't see the ewe turn.

What do ducks watch on TV?
Duckumentaries.

Knock, knock.
Who's there?
Interrupting cow.
Interrup..
MOO!

Knock, knock.
Who's there?
Cows go.
Cows go who?
Cows go moo.

HONK!

Why do cows wear bells?
Because their horns don't work.

Where do cows dance?
At the meatball.

How do you count cows?
With a cowculator!

What do you get if
you cross a dinosaur
with a pig?
Jurassic pork!

What do you call a
pony with a sore throat?
A little horse.

Did you hear the one about the farmer?
He was outstanding in his field.

What do you get if you cross a clown with a goat? A silly billy.

What do pigs put on sore feet? Oinkment.

What do you call a sheep with no legs? A cloud.

What do you get if you cross a karate expert with a pig? Pork chops.

What happened when the cow tried to jump over the fence? It was an udder catastrophe.

JOKING CATS AND DOGS

What's worse than raining cats and dogs?
Hailing taxis.

When is the vet busiest?
When it's raining cats and dogs.

Have you heard the story
about the cat on the roof?
Don't worry about it, it's
over your head.

CHOMP!

JOKES, JOKES AND MORE JOKES

PUP CORN

What is a dog's favourite snack?
Pupcorn.

Ten cats were on a boat and one jumped off. How many were left? None, they were all copycats.

Where do you find a dog with no legs? Right where you left him.

What do you give a dog with a fever? Mustard – it's the best thing for a hot dog.

What kind of cat cuts grass? A lawn meower.

What does a cat eat when it's hot?
Mice cream.

What kind of cereal do cats eat?
Mice crispies!

MUNCH!
CRUNCH!

MICE CRISPIES

What do you call a dog that gets mail?
A golden receiver.

What dog keeps the best time?
A watch dog.

SCHOOL DAZE

Sarah: "My teacher yelled at me today for something I didn't do."
Sophie: "What was that?"
Sarah: "My homework."

Teacher: "Simon, can you spell your name backwards?"
Simon: "No mis."

Teacher: "When you go in the bathroom you're British, when you leave the bathroom you're British. What are you IN the bathroom?"
David: "European!"

Teacher: "Which two days of the week start with the letter 'T'?"
Simon: "Today and tomorrow!"

Why did the teacher write the lesson on the window?
He wanted it to be very clear.

Is a hammer a good tool for maths class?
No, you need multi-pliers.

Why were the teacher's eyes crossed?
She couldn't control her pupils.